WHAT I SHOULD HAVE SAID

A Poetry Memoir
about Losing a Child
to Addiction

poems by

Lanette Sweeney

Featuring poetry by her late son,
Kyle Fisher-Hertz

Finishing Line Press
Georgetown, Kentucky

WHAT I SHOULD HAVE SAID

*A Poetry Memoir
about Losing a Child
to Addiction*

Publisher: Leah Huete de Maines

Editor: Christen Kincaid

Original Cover Photo: Zachary Matthay

Cover Design is by Lanette Sweeney with assistance from Joshua Hertz and Debra Meltzer Mezaros.

Author photo inside: Laura Hunter

Photo of author and son on back taken by author.

Order online: www.finishinglinepress.com
            also available at local bookstores, Bookshop.org and Amazon.com

Author inquiries and mail orders:
Finishing Line Press
P. O. Box 1626
Georgetown, Kentucky 40324
U. S. A.

Table of Contents

A TRAGEDY TOLD THROUGH THE STAGES OF GRIEF

DENIAL & DEPRESSION

Getting the News 1

Eulogy for Faith 3

Eleven... 5

Puberty by Kyle Fisher-Hertz, age 11 6

Safety Plan 7

Before We Were Afraid Our Son Would Rob Us.............................9

Problem Child by Kyle Fisher-Hertz, age 12 11

Adriana 14

Let's Watch The Sunrise by Kyle Fisher-Hertz, age 18........................ 16

Masterpiece 17

Mother's Day Sonnet by Kyle Fisher-Hertz, age 23 18

Each Day My Death Draws Nearer by Kyle Fisher-Hertz, age 20 19

The Greatest of These 20

Our First Date by Kyle Fisher-Hertz, age 20.................. 21

Dance by Kyle Fisher-Hertz, age 22............................23

For My Son on His 18th Birthday 24

Irreconcilable 25

Application Supplication by Kyle Fisher-Hertz, age 25..................... 26

Second Deadly Sin... 27

ANGER

Thanksgiving 2017 31

We Wanted You to Know We Trusted You...............................32

All Our Hope Got Us Here...33

Zombie.. 34

Here's What They Mean 35

I Was Born Kyle by Kyle Fisher-Hertz, age 21 37

Villanelle For The Night My Mother Found My Son
    Standing Over Her Bed...38
Sleep It Off by Kyle Fisher-Hertz, age 19 39
What You Learned at Rehab 40
Rehab Rap by Kyle Fisher-Hertz, age 25 41
May His Memory Be For a Blessing...44
Toxic by Kyle Fisher-Hertz, age 23..45
Snake Charmer 46
Other Mothers 47
I Rue the Nights by Kyle Fisher-Hertz, age 23.............................49
Vows 50
I Don't Know How You Do It...51
Liquor Bottle Might As Well Be A Pistol by Kyle Fisher-Hertz,
    age 25..52
Unsolicited Advice 53
Everything Happens 54
Black and White...55

BARGAINING
Thanksgiving 2018 59
Reversing Time...61
Things I Did That I Imagine Killed My Son....................................63
My Life Is A Boring Tragedy by Kyle Fisher-Hertz, age 25 64
Dust...65
Could I Have Kept You Here? 66
The Only High by Kyle Fisher-Hertz, age 25................................67
Sliding Doors 68
Many Mothers Make Worse Mistakes 69
Pressure Resistant 70
Without You by Kyle Fisher-Hertz, age 24....................................71
Another Morning Breaks 72
What I Should Have Said 73
Cold Comfort 74

Echo..75
That Moment by Kyle Fisher-Hertz, age 22 77
Beautiful Boy..78
For Amber by Kyle Fisher-Hertz, age 26 79
Don't Go 81
Vegas by Kyle Fisher-Hertz, age 24 82
Forensic Examination 83

ACCEPTANCE & FINDING MEANING
Thanksgiving 2002 by Kyle Fisher-Hertz, age 11 87
Reliquary 88
I Never Wanted My Fortune Told 89
Crocodile by Kyle Fisher-Hertz, age 24 90
The Body's Expression 91
Natural Wonders 94
For Those Who Need Science Before Faith 95
Unplugged by Kyle Fisher-Hertz, age 24 97
Learning to Live Together 98
The Speed of Life 99
A Lesson From Amanda Palmer's Podcast 100
Acceptance 101
The Burn Mosaic 102
Right Here by Kyle Fisher-Hertz, age 26............................103
My Mother Knows Death and Its Lessons 104
I Fear That My Prayers by Kyle Fisher-Hertz, age 26........105
Contributing 106
Breaking Down at Cape Neddick.......................................107
List of Hopes 108

AFTERWORD 109
ACKNOWLEDGMENTS 111

This collection is dedicated to
Maggie Jean Cockrell, my granddaughter and Kyle's daughter.
We are your family.

A TRAGEDY TOLD THROUGH
THE STAGES OF GRIEF

DENIAL
AND
DEPRESSION

GETTING THE NEWS

The night that bled into the morning my son died,
my phone rang at 2 a.m. I resisted picking up, but soon
heard my mother's frantic message—my son, living with her,
had run off, was using, had left his daughter and girlfriend
behind. I lay awake until morning refusing to call back,
sure my dramatic mother was causing me useless terror.

Bleary-eyed, I went to work, called my therapist, as if
she could help, called my ex-husband to say our son
was missing. We agreed to hope he was in jail. When
my mother called again, I picked up, ready to scold
her hysteria, and heard, "Lanette, he's dead." "No," I said,
an echo of every mother on this call. "No. No. No. No."

"Yes," she said, "the police are here." I sank down screaming
like an animal set on fire. Co-workers came running, faces
mirrored masks of horror. The cops had my son's wallet
but refused to answer my mother's question: "Is he dead?"
For ten minutes, they questioned her like a suspect; still ten
better than all minutes after. I hoped his wallet had been stolen.

His girlfriend, blonde hair swinging, came out clutching their
two-year-old, demanding, "What the fuck is wrong with you?
Why couldn't you answer her the first time?" *Standard procedure*,
they said. Not how families got the news in any movie we'd seen.
I needed to get to my daughter, wanted to tell her in person,
to catch her when she fell down. I phoned my husband.

He no longer felt like my ex. "Really?" he asked, bewildered,
despite our years of holding our breath. I called a friend, asked
him to look after my husband, but he told his wife, a teacher
my son called Mama Laurie, and she collapsed in class. Word
spread. My daughter called while I was in line to get on the plane.
"I got a crazy call," she said, "Someone heard a rumor Kyle died."

I hesitated, wanting to leave her in the land of before. She heard it.
"He's dead?" she asked. "Wait," I pleaded. "I'm boarding now."

Then no more words, just her far-off shrieks. We flew together
to the body in the Vegas coroner's office. They wouldn't let me
see it. "It's autopsied," they warned. "His scalp is cut off."
I didn't care; I needed to see his face. Only then did I believe.

EULOGY FOR FAITH

"Today I'll walk another day without you.
I'll carry you in me, like before you were born."
—Sheryl St. Germaine, *The Small Door of Your Death*

Born blue with a whorl
on his scalp, he had to be coaxed
to draw in his first breath while
the doctor stitched me together.

I watched peacefully; I knew
he'd come swirling in to be mine.

When he was two, awaiting
his sister's birth, he told me
he remembered his own:
"I was wet," he said, "and cold."

As a toddler, he talked to God every night,
mystifying us, his agnostic parents. His God
looked like the fairy godmother in Disney's
Cinderella, was always there to chat.

How could I be scared
in the face of such natural faith?

He carried his tiny teddy everywhere:
Tooka Took. He had tea parties for stuffies,
rubbed his sister's peach-fuzz head each time
he ran by her, their love his touchstone.

He started preschool shy and sweet,
but by first grade developed a taste
for the thrill of rule-breaking. Wrote
"fuck" on a bathroom wall just for fun.

His love of looking for trouble seemed
mostly harmless; I had full faith in him.

A teacher's aide sent him to the library to keep
his busy mind occupied, bade him learn of Icarus,
who soared toward the sun but refused to heed
parental warnings, fell from the sky, and died.

We couldn't see he was studying
his autobiography.

He did math with the Talented-Gifted kids
years older. He won the DARE poetry prize:
a stuffed lion. He gave up training wheels,
played T-ball, soccer, basketball, hockey,

practiced telling jokes on top of a windy hill
to make sure his voice carried, then won
local talent shows, looked for louder applause,
joined a comedy troupe, festivals, got on TV.

Then, on *America's Got Talent*, he was called
a talentless high-school nerd by the talentless
Piers Morgan and never went on stage again,
began stashing weed inside his prize lion.

Fear settled too late in me. His fate
was sealed by the time I woke up, terrified.

There are infinite ways to tell this story,
but they all start and end the same way:
Born without breath, brought back to life,
beloved beyond measure, buoyant, airborne.

Then his teddy bear lost, his faith
shattered, his chariot incinerated,
his beautiful body burnt, turned to ashes
buried in a box in my backyard.

Now I'm in a permanent panic; I became
a nervous wreck as soon as I couldn't reach him.

ELEVEN

He was a ring bearer
in a tiny, tailored
three-piece suit.
At his cousin's
rehearsal dinner,
he shared a goofy
poem about dreading
puberty, then one
about love. We square-
danced, full of joy
all night. Once home,
his puberty began.

He watched me give up
on his father, break up
his home, move him
cross country and back.
When we replanted him
in familiar soil, instead of
happy, he turned angry,
his pranks less funny,
his arrogance blooming.

He seemed to steer back
on track, got an agent,
a pilot on Nickelodeon,
told jokes on big stages.

But nothing ever beat 11,
when his shine was
undimmed by shadows,
his mind clear, his heart
unbroken; when he still knew
he could do anything.

PUBERTY

by Kyle Fisher-Hertz, age 11

Growing up, growing up, growing up fast:
Puberty's finally here at last!
I'm so excited about becoming a man;
Puberty sounds like a pretty good plan.

Wait, what's that you say?
My whole body will change?
My voice will get deeper
and sound very strange?

And by the end of each day
I'll be drenched in sweat
and there'll be different
deodorants I'll have to get?

And sometimes I'll have
wet dreams with no warning
and wake up wet and sticky
in the morning?

And I'll get big pimples
that I'll have to pop?
I think I want this
growing-up stuff to STOP!

A clip of 11-year-old Kyle reciting this poem can be seen here:
https://youtu.be/qEUZtTs_u-A

SAFETY PLAN

When you were a small boy,
safe in superhero pajamas,
you were inexplicably afraid
a bad man would break in,
steal you from your bed—
or that the rest of us
would be killed, and you
left alone and defenseless.

You woke from nightmares
of scary men climbing
in the window, hiding in the car,
sneaking in with a gun.
We didn't know how or why
in our suburban townhouse
where you slept surrounded
by stuffed animals
you'd dreamed up this terror.

You wanted a safety plan.
"But what *if* a man broke in?
What if he had a gun?
What would you do?"
You insisted we imagine our way
out of the unlikeliest situations.

My father was a heroin addict,
dead at 24,
and now you are a heroin addict
dead at 26.

Why didn't we make a safety plan
for the monster I knew
might be lying in wait
in your genes?
Why was I so sure of your safety,
making light of your terror,

promising you nothing and no one
could ever take you away
from the circle of love
in which we put you to bed each night?

BEFORE WE WERE AFRAID
OUR SON WOULD ROB US

For twenty years
we never locked our doors.

Once a man stumbled in
at 3 a.m., drunk and confused.
My husband found him asleep
on the couch in the morning,
He left meekly, filling the room
with sheepish apologies.

Once a fragile boy
who needed sober parents
snuck into our bedroom
and stole the pipe and
small bag of pot I kept
in a shoe box in my closet.
I felt sadder he'd discovered
I did drugs, like his mother,
than that he'd stolen from me.

Once a neighbor's kid
crept in and carried off
my son's video games.
He was playing them
when we confronted his mother
at their door. "Motherhood
has been a thankless job,"
she said, handing them back.
I couldn't imagine then
what she meant.

None of these intrusions
was enough to change
the lazy ease with which
we left our lives exposed.
We trusted; we possessed
nothing of greater value

than the sense of safety
we felt knowing none of us
ever needed to carry a key.

Our door was always open.

PROBLEM CHILD

by Kyle Fisher-Hertz, age 12

You might ask yourself:
How dare I say this?
I have no right to be pissed.
I'm just a child—
a wild child,
a child who wants to be riled
Up
but instead I'm filed
Down.
Down by people who are meant
to keep us down,
to squelch our imagination,
any new creation
that comes from innovation
so that we may "enjoy"
the freedom of this nation
precisely the way they want us to.

We call these people: Teachers.
Now don't get me wrong,
there are teachers who are strong,
who want to see us grow,
who teach us
what we really need to know,
but there are teachers who are weak
who completely freak
at anything unique
easily molding and folding
those who are meek.

And those who are stronger?
They just take longer.
But they too will be broken like the others,
like their fathers and their mothers
and their sisters and their brothers.
Except for a few

who just say no
who won't go with the flow
because they know
if they take this bullshit
that's being hawked up
and spit in their faces
and just stand
in their respective spaces
that they'll be hypnotized
and they'll get that
glazed over look in their eyes.
So they don't. They won't.
They refuse. They won't be used
and so they are labeled
Problem Children.

And so they write on my report
Where I can't possibly retort,
"Student disrupts class;
interferes with the learning of others."

Disrupt? Ha! Please!
If I wanted to DISrupt, I would E-rupt
I would get up on my desk and scream:
Everyone! RUN! RUN! RUN!
GET OUT OF HERE, PROTECT YOUR BRAIN,
LEAVE BEFORE WE ALL GO INSANE!"
I would get a roomful of blank stares
And I would realize
I was too late.
But that's not my style.
I don't disrupt.
I enlighten, brighten, heighten
the learning of others
in an attempt to start a revolution
and stop the pollution
of our minds
so we don't all grow up
in a single file line

taking whatever we get
and saying, "Oh, that's fine."

So it's up to you:
Let them take over YOUR mind,
but not mine. Never mine:
I am a proud Problem Child.

ADRIANA

The summer between
your troubled high-school finish
and your start at the state school
sure to save you from yourself
you were a camp counselor;
kids clung to you like barnacles.

You fell hard for a 27-year-old
Brazilian there for the summer.
Nine years your senior, Adriana
eyed you with open admiration.

She was made gorgeous by being crazy
about you, eager to show you
how to have sex like a grown-up.

After a month you wanted
to marry her, to help her stay.
We begged you to go to college,
live as planned in a dorm—where
you quickly fell into old patterns
with new friends, life at school
the same rolling party
you'd vowed to leave behind.

What if we hadn't stopped you?
What if you knew you'd do better
as a young newlywed, coming home
to be with your bride, Adriana, whose
Skype calls you answered less and less
as your college wasteland took over?

You knew you needed another way
through life, a way to escape from
yourself and the well-worn path
we'd planted you on. I'm sorry
we kept sending you back whenever

you veered, sorry for all our efforts
to keep you right where we thought
you needed to be. What did we know?

LET'S WATCH THE SUNRISE

A Poem About Adriana by Kyle Fisher-Hertz, age 18

We lay on the side of a hill,
that may have been moist with morning dew.
The birds chirped their early chatter.
They might have sung anything.

My arm lay beneath your shoulders while
my fingers danced a caress across your arm.
The breath of your kiss tickled my ear
and I smiled as I rolled you on top of me,
and took your lower lip between mine.

Just then the first rays of the sun hurdled the horizon
and raced toward us across the lake.
Or maybe it was ten minutes from then.
Or maybe the sun never rose that morning,
but instead appeared all at once in the sky,
the moment the wake-up bell rang,
and we had to hurry back to our cabins.

MASTERPIECE

I thought you'd always think like me
(minus the insecurity).
I thought the womb in which you grew
spun my filaments into you,
then left a tether, light as floss,
to ground you if you wandered off.

I hoped I'd only passed along
the genes that made you smart and strong:
a matching smile, a laugh contagious,
a tendency to act outrageous.
I couldn't see we also shared
a drowning pull toward deep despair.

I believed, like me, you'd find your way—
you'd scale some cliffs but then belay.
So when I saw you climbing higher,
I lay myself beneath the wire.
I thought, like me, you'd be afraid
to ruin the masterpiece we'd made.

Instead you leapt toward empty space
and smashed each cell. My heart, my face,
the fevered head I held and kissed,
you flung that, too, toward the abyss.
You tore the tether from my hand,
no thoughts, like mine, of where you'd land.

MOTHER'S DAY SONNET

by Kyle Fisher-Hertz, age 23

The all we see is less than what we know.
The lens extends the more one understands.
Reality is shaped by how we grow.
The world I know you formed with gentle hands.

You mothered my perception into being,
and paved my path with truths on which to move.
And still they echo in the world I'm seeing.
"Be kind," and "love," and "leave the world improved."

As I traverse beyond the groove you laid,
I keep my view, yet see how others see.
I realize what a masterpiece you've made.
This world that seems so real's unique to me.

This point of view you've built, I'd want no other
You've shined your light on life just right, my mother.

EACH DAY MY DEATH DRAWS NEARER

by Kyle Fisher-Hertz, age 20

Each day my death draws nearer than the last.
I say this not in fear but just in fact.
No sense to cry and say that life's too fast.
Although it sometimes helps to just look back.

Reflection really is a vital tool
to see the sorrows suffered years before.
But holding grudges keeps you more a fool.
Recalling with forgiveness opens doors.

To keep our foes in mind will chill the soul.
It's better to accept and just let go.
We must forgive each other as a whole.
This is the only way we'll ever grow.

This time spent looking back has clearly shown
the sins I must forgive: my own.

THE GREATEST OF THESE

For two years I thought love was your lifeboat
as you created the life of your dreams:
you taught math, played Frisbee, sold sperm, worked hard,
mountain climbed to fill your need for extremes.

Steph tells me now she could always see signs
of the demons you kept lying in wait,
the six packs you drank while she sipped her wines,
the coke, the molly, the bills you paid late.

You told me Steph replaced your addictions;
she was, for a while, your one desire—
until you chafed at dreamed-up restrictions
to your new goal of just getting higher.

Why couldn't you remember how lonely
you got when left with your one and only?

OUR FIRST DATE

For Steph by Kyle Fisher-Hertz, age 20

They say that at the dawn of time itself, before the Big Bang,
all the matter in the universe was squished together into a single point.

Which means that every atom that forms and fills you today
was there in that sliver of space before time began.
And so was I.
And there we floated, timelessly.
Entangled with impossible closeness.

Annoyingly, everyone else in the universe
was also there crowding our space,
but I am sure that our subatomic particles just cuddled
and made snarky comments to each other
about how absurd and awkward they all looked
hunching and smushing each other to fit into that singularity,
and you laughed.

You know your laugh elicits my kisses,
but back then it did not, for a kiss did not exist.
My lips could not come closer. Your mouth was already wrapped in mine.
Our fingers caressed each other ceaselessly, everywhere at once.
Affection was the constant of our existence.

But then, alas, the universe began.
With terrifying abruptness
Space replaced our embrace with a bang.
We were pried and flung from each other,
Sent screaming out into the universe.
And you looked at me desperately
before we both dissipated alone into the emptiness.

It took 14 billion years for our particles to reassemble in the form of you and me.
Enough time that we had all but forgotten the connection that once bound us.
So when we met again, the image of you wafted through my eyes,
like an ex-lover's perfume whose scent I couldn't quite place.
When you first spoke, your voice transcended seduction.

It entranced my cells, and began to wake me from a dream I'd mistaken as life.
On a sweaty subway car, we stood for our stop and you stumbled slightly.
And at last I grasped your hand.
And as the open doors let in the June breeze,
I felt the whole universe exhale in relief.

DANCE

For Steph By Kyle Fisher-Hertz, age 22

Little more than a year ago, I was a sixth grader and you were an eighth grader, my hands on your hips at a middle school dance. We allowed ourselves to draw closer than any other circumstances would have permitted, because we knew no matter how close we got, our dance would be over by the end of the song. But as the melodic Brooklyn summer song played on, and our stiff-armed rocking melted into an embracing sway, our eye contact grew so intense that I finally lost balance and fell into the depth of your pupils into a plane where nothing existed but us.

When my feet finally touched solid ground again, I was a man with his hands on the love of his life and I was suddenly aware that innumerable songs had begun and ended since I first took your hand in mine, but all had followed the synchronized tempo of our beating hearts, and I knew then we would dance for the rest of our lives.

FOR MY SON ON HIS 18TH BIRTHDAY

When you were a baby and a soft, small boy,
it was easy to show how I treasured you,
kissing each tiny toe, sweet as a corn kernel,
blowing silly sounds on your powdery belly,
dancing you in circles in the living room,
playing hide and seek, whiffle ball, tag,
letting you catch me, every time.

There was nothing
you wanted then
that I couldn't give you.

When your body hardened and grew away from me,
it was harder to show how I adored you,
harder to hold you, harder to kiss
your keppy or soothe you, make you giggle,
get you to write poetry or watch stars,
harder to find a game you would play
that you didn't win every time.

There was nothing
you wanted anymore
that I could give you.

Now that you're a man I have to reach up to hug,
I hope you'll let me show you again
how precious you are, let me go back
to believing in you the way I always did before
you tried to make me stop. Let me laugh
at your jokes and cheer for your
hopes and give advice when you're afraid.

Even though now
everything you want
only you can give you.

IRRECONCILABLE

Here is my sweet-faced boy—
polite, attentive, anxious
to please, making up

for the men he was ashamed
to show me, the dirty joker,
the one who dreaded waking up.

Now that he's disappeared,
I'm left reconciling his
unbalanced checkbook.

Was he an earnest, eager helper,
first to do dishes in a friend's home,
slow-motion runner in kiddie tag?

Or a foolish disciple of *Jackass,*
biking slowly in front of cars,
luring cops to his first arrest?

Too sweet to be a ladies' man,
friend-zoned, tender romantic,
penning rejected sonnets?

Or callously cruel,
too lazy to use condoms,
notching scores as he came?

Who was he? I fear he died
without knowing how few of us
ever reconcile our many selves.

APPLICATION SUPPLICATION

by Kyle Fisher-Hertz, age 25

in response to a job ad asking applicants to send in a video

I'm a nerd from the burbs who spits hot fire,
and to be sure I'm a worker that you wanna acquire.
I'll show up 10 minutes early in the proper attire,
and if you doubt my product knowledge, go ahead and inquire.

I've never been fired 'cause I'm so pleasant to work with:
communicate effectively, somewhat of a wordsmith.
Never heard the word lazy; that would be an absurd dis.

A first kiss is like my work
—it's filled with passion.
I'm a self-starter,
motivate myself to action,
and once these actions gain traction,
distractions get no reaction,
nor am I crashin',
I've got the passion of some fanatical faction.
I just keep going
like a number not expressed by a fraction,
so I'm only irrational
if a math question is asking.

All that to say, when I'm focused I'm all deep.
And I manage a task like control-alt-delete,
so I'll complete this rap with a plea:
Brick Gym, please, you've gotta interview me.

Video of Kyle reading this poem can be seen at
https://www.youtube.com/watch?v=H_y43XmXHHY

SECOND DEADLY SIN
A Broken Ghazal

When I see a woman reaching to embrace her grown son
I ache to wrap my arms around your broad shoulders, dear one.

Instead, I have to turn my face before it comes undone,
reveals my envy of mothers who love a living son.

I wanted daughters; when pregnant was scared I'd have a son;
then you came, baby boy, taught me how to love from day one.

You laughed at stories of chariot races toward the sun;
kept me in stitches, made jokes of disasters, funny one,

until suddenly the laughter died; I saw you'd begun
to turn into the monster in your own story, my son.

I fought to save you, Kyle, can't believe the monster won.
With your body gone, how can I not covet every other one.

ANGER

THANKSGIVING, 2017

For my son, who died six weeks before the 2016 election

You got out just in time to avoid the fires,
the furies, the floods, the shamings,
the shams, the cyclones, the shifting sands.

You flipped a switch as you went, turning
the whole world dark, our lives collapsing
with millions of newly minted mourners'.

The apocalypse is just a macabre metaphor
for what is happening here, the rapid melt
of icecaps and civility rushing us to the end.

You didn't leave a note, just a mess and membership
in the largest self-induced death club in history,
brightest boys leaping like lemmings off the ledge.

Where is the guide for survivors: how to swim
through a tsunami, how to hike a scorched-earth
trail of tears, how to shop on through the end times.

Now for Thanksgiving, our bounty holds us hostage,
our gratitude a savage hook through our noses
reminding us of all we still have to lose. Let us pray.

WE WANTED YOU TO KNOW WE TRUSTED YOU

We knew you weren't like the other addicts,
the ones whose parents wouldn't see them;
we left our purses and pockets unattended,
tried not to worry when you stayed too long
in bathrooms, when spoons disappeared, cash.

When VISA phoned, waking me to say my card
was being used at a 7-11 to buy tank after tank,
I thought it stolen, realized with a gut-punch:
it was you, getting people to give you cash for
their gas as you charged my card again and again.

We knew you weren't like the other addicts,
the ones whose families had given up on them.
We'd given you my credit card, watched you
sign up for student loans, sent you money
so you could go to meetings every night.

You used us and crack until you ran through
all the student-loan money, couldn't see how
you still got an A in your science course
(white privilege, that's how, we see now),
sold your PlayStation to sit alone in a haze.

We could have saved ourselves time and worry
if we'd believed you as soon as you showed us
you were like the other addicts: Couldn't be trusted
to pick up our prescriptions, were poised to lift bills
from our piggybanks, pilfer our pills as we slept.

We just wanted you to be,
unlike the other addicts,
someone we could trust.

ALL OUR HOPE GOT US HERE

My keep-'em-laughing,
cupid-lipped son died at 26,
overdosed on a Best Western
bathroom floor. He kept a
promise to me by wearing
his bike helmet to ride there.
Beforehand, he took out the
trash for his grandma, said
he was sorry he couldn't stay.

Seven weeks later,
I watched, slack-jawed,
as Trump's firstborn son
held up the bloody stump
of an elephant's tail, boasted
of the bull market, tweeted
support of tyrants—"I love it!"

Meanwhile, my firstborn son,
who wrote sonnets and taught
4th graders long division and
self-esteem and fell to his knees
praying to help people, not hurt
them, is just one more dead junkie
in a nation awash in dying addicts.

My son's daughter is fatherless,
Trump her nation's father-in-chief.
False encouragement once seemed
better than none, but now I believe
it more important to bear witness
to this end of days in which
we are trapped, flies in molasses,
wings beating uselessly as the bile
we regurgitate softens our last,
sticky sips at the poisoned trough.

ZOMBIE

Zombie stories show our infected loved ones
moving toward us hungrily. Familiar faces
flood us with feeling before we catch sight
of who they've become, their deadly appetite

eating them alive as they turn their gaze on us.
How to run when it's my son, begging me
to take him in, morphing before me, scratching
off chunks of his flesh, fresh wounds oozing.

The light in his eyes drains to empty, yet still
I'm determined to drag him back from the undead,
don't want to see his soul is gone, though his body
staggers on. The happy end of a zombie tale

is supposed to be our escape before the soulless
sink their teeth in. But how to survive when
the voice we adore howls for help we don't have?
How to ignore the desperate pounding at the door?

HERE'S WHAT THEY MEAN

When they smile and
tell you to enjoy them
while they're young,

They mean, "Enjoy believing
the long days you endure
tantrums and scrub shit
from that rug you chose
when you were expecting,
all the deep breaths you took
and the calm you kept
when the bed was wet
and the glasses broken,
all your hunting for just-right
day care, all your lavish praise,
will all pay off on some future day.

Enjoy the great parenting lie:
it's all worth it in the end!
(Don't count costs.)
Enjoy your unshaken faith
that labors of love
will deliver the child
you always wanted.

"Enjoy them while they're
still blank, unsullied slates
onto which you can project
a montage of perfection.
Enjoy them while
their shocking rudeness
still makes you laugh,
before they glare, sneer,
hurt people—on purpose—
give up, fit in, glaze over,
tell lies, get high, slam by,
destroy your every

fantasy of who you
dreamed they'd be.

"Enjoy your naiveté.
Enjoy imagining
there's a finish line
or it's ever getting easier."

I WAS BORN "KYLE"

by Kyle Fisher-Hertz, age 21

I was born "Kyle."

It was the first of many things my parents gave me,
chosen with consideration and love.
Kyle was a vision of the future in my parents' minds,
blurry, but vibrantly colored.

As they raised me, they nurtured and molded
the Kyle they named into existence,
but as years passed, and my identity's clay
became more my own to mold,
I was the predestined Kyle less and less,
and a beast of my own creation more and more.

VILLANELLE FOR THE NIGHT MY MOTHER FOUND MY SON STANDING OVER HER BED

For this to be the outcome: a dead-eyed sociopath
who lies, steals, and cares only for his next fix…
Why did I pour so much love into every bath?

Did I review spelling words, cheer him on in math,
teach him to play Scrabble, practice soccer kicks
for this to be the outcome: a dead-eyed sociopath?

Should I have scolded more? Not held back my wrath?
Not applauded jokes and puppet shows and magic tricks?
Why did I pour so much love into every bath?

Why did I get training wheels to help him on his path?
Why sleepless nights, why adenoid surgery at six
for this to be the outcome: a dead-eyed sociopath?

Why helmets? Why hiking? Why carefully charted growth?
Why did I make him eat all those fucking carrot sticks?
Why did I pour so much love into every bath?

Why can't he see me drowning in his aftermath?
Did I make him think there was nothing he couldn't fix
for this to be the outcome: a dead-eyed sociopath?
Why did I pour so much love into every bath?

SLEEP IT OFF

By Kyle Fisher-Hertz, age 19

Bees buzz just inches from the water's surface,
Ready to sting the moment I emerge to take a breath.
But as fresh memory-scars begin to pierce my morning dream,
I grow gills and swim deep into the darkness,
Desperate to stay submerged.

WHAT YOU LEARNED AT REHAB

After you got thrown out
of the Vegas rehab treating you
for free because of your zeal
for recovery, you turned your rage
on us. You screamed at your sister
for not getting her shoes on quicker,
filled me with terror as I sped you
to work. You swore we were making
you late, might get you fired, then
left me open-mouthed as you climbed
from the car, lit a leisurely cigarette,
sauntered off to slowly smoke it
instead of running to punch in.

I knew then you needed real help,
help beyond drug counseling, help
for your insane, explosive anger,
but I took what I could get, feeling
lucky to get anything. I had to beg
the insurance counselors; their rules
said crack use wasn't good enough
to earn you inpatient coverage.
"Crack can't kill him," one argued,
"He doesn't need detox from crack,
and rehab only comes after detox."
I wept. I shouted, "Does he need
to start using needles right now
before you'll get him some help?"

So they relented, got you in,
the only one there not yet on heroin.
No therapy, lots of 12-step meetings.
In at last, you finally met the men
who showed you how to shoot up,
who taught you about all the highs
you'd been missing on the outside.

REHAB BATTLE RAP

by Kyle Fisher-Hertz, age 25

You want to rap-battle me?
I'll slaughter you like cattle, G.
Me and what army?
My vocabulary's [my] cavalry!
My hands're behind my back,
you fuckin' hack.
Come take a jab at me.
'cause I'm a verbal boxer.
[My] words'll outfox you.
Stop dodgin'—whap—
I'll spit shit that rocks you,
drops you to sleep so deep
you'll wake up with bed sores.

Look around—
see red sheets and red floors.
At the edge of your bed,
see the head of a dead horse.
That's my Godfather ploy,
[I] extort cash, so send yours
while I punch this pony
that just jumped from 10 floors.
Get it? That's beating a dead horse.
With all these punchlines
about dead equine,
it's redundant,
But it's abundantly clear
that I'll mind-fuck you raw
'til I come in your ear.

Oh, here comes your girl;
I suggest you keep her near, son,
lest my revered tongue
slither up in her eardrum
and spit soliloquies
so fierce her ears come.

She's feeling what this nerd say,
'cause Friday through Thursday
I'll send my rhymes to recess
'cause I'm obsessed
with wordplay.
I'll spray you down with verbs and nouns
and sting you like a salted cut.
I snack on other rappers.
Run your trap; you'll be assaulted, nut.

My subject's my jab,
my right hook's my predicate,
I'll throw a combination
that'll leave your ego edited.
Forget it, kid; I'm credited
on streets and universities.
My fire burns your ass to ash;
the burns you dish are first-degree.
Oh mercy me, the worst of me
comes out to get the best of you.
For you to be a-head,
Must mean I chopped it off the rest of you,

And that's just a few bars you can't digest,
'cause I serve it up too quickly,
like a lunch lady on meth.
You're just a hungry sucker,
like a baby on a breast.
Well, blow into a piggy bank.
Save your breath
cause you['re] about to need it—
you['re] defeated and you['re] breathless,
you crashed, you['re] a dummy .

Now you know not to test this.
I'm a balanced breakfast;
you're five soggy Apple Jacks.
Am I the best? Fact!
You can slap that on a Snapple cap,

Invasive species, nothing eats me
in this habitat. Apex predator.
—[I'm the] T-rex of battle rap.

Video of Kyle performing this rap in his last rehab can be seen here:
https://youtu.be/UK14Ar2uS6E

MAY HIS MEMORY BE FOR A BLESSING

"The evil that men do lives after them;
The good is oft interred with their bones."
—William Shakespeare, *Julius Caesar*

I hate that the stories I most often recall
cast light on your most demoralized days;
moments your values plunged into freefall
play on repeat for me, make false my praise.

I'd rather recall how you found that wad—
thousands in cash you saw drop roadside.
Homeless, yet still you gave chase, pedaled hard,
returned the whole stack, felt one moment's pride.

But what matter that often you did right—
when you were a deadbeat who drove your kid high?
Your 2-year-old watched you nod each night,
her howls rising as you crawled off to die.

How to find blessings in your memory
when you monstrous moments keep haunting me?

TOXIC

By Kyle Fisher-Hertz, age 23

Like a new mother in a crowd with her child,
I grip tight and refuse to release.
But despite my focused clutch, I feel my grip start to slip,
and I know then, this foulness inside me will soon emerge.
I beg a God I don't believe in to please
keep it inside me, to keep this bubbling ugliness from escaping,
at least a little while longer.
I can't let it surface, not in front of her.
Her beautiful lips speak to me, oblivious to the toxicity hidden within.
And then, right in the middle of her sentence,
I lose control.
I see an all-too-familiar disgust take over her face,
and a minute later she leaves my room and my life forever.
In the sad, sickening silence that remains,
I open a window and vow to never eat a burrito
on a first date again.

SNAKE CHARMER

Freshly arrived at the home of a friend
who took him in off the streets,
he posts photos for the world to see
how he charms his next victim.

He smiles into her eyes,
their bodies touch as they sit close,
gaze rapturously at one another,
all problems, debts, arrests behind him.

The baby he hasn't seen yet in person
is four months old, 3,000 miles away.
He has no photos with his unmet child,
but these pics he finds time to post.

The friend gives him a job and a home.
He gets jumped buying himself smack,
but tells her he was mugged buying her
marijuana, so she buys him a new bike.

He shoots up in a park, then has
unprotected sex with this friend.
They're both desperate for connection;
plus, he says, he's afraid to disappoint her.

When she throws him out, puts his stuff
on the street, she writes to tell me
how hurt she is, but how she hopes
he's going to be OK. She's worried.

Two years later, this friend sits with us
as we weep at his funeral. She wouldn't
give him a reference for a job,
but she's stricken that he ran out of luck.

He had that effect on all of us,
snake charmer that he was. We all of us
forgot everything he'd done, believed
in him utterly when he looked in our eyes.

OTHER MOTHERS

Don't come asking for my advice
then mask your ask as sympathy.
Don't act as if you're playing nice
by pawing through my tragedy.

Don't tell me you're just wondering
what I've learned since my son died,
You're shameless with your plundering
of my destroyed maternal pride.

Don't tell me you've given warnings
you're sure *your* children will heed.
You're still in your kids' bright mornings;
who knows where their troubles might lead?

Or maybe your judgment is based
on successfully raised adults.
You're sure if I'd done it your way,
I would have had better results.

I used to judge just like you all,
believed I'd earned my good fortune.
Thought my steps prevented a fall,
thought life dealt pain in fair portion.

My son lived, not died, because of me,
I did not make him an addict.
But with suicide or an O.D.
other mothers *hope* I slackened.

Who wants to believe that nothing
can save children set on a course?
What mom doesn't think her loving
is safeguarding her from a loss?

So fine, hold on to your belief.
Just don't pretend you're curious.

when comforting someone in grief,
fake questions make us furious.

Here's all we've learned: Suffering's real,
and nothing we do prevents it.
Lives upend with the spin of a wheel.
Please say we're blameless—as if you meant it.

I RUE THE NIGHTS

by Kyle Fisher-Hertz, age 23

The nights (more than the days) I rue,
reflected on in morning light
the shadows of the nights are true.
I shield my eyes when skies are blue,
and keep them squinted 'til the night.
The nights (more than the days) I rue.
I feed my wants at every cue,
with disregard as if of spite.
The shadows of the nights are true.
Details; I try not to review.
But flood and drown me in insight.
The nights (more than the days) I rue.
I rue… But what good does it do
if only when the world is bright
the shadows of the nights are true?

VOWS

Sixteen days before you died, a woman
I used to be wore white lace with pink petals
and stood before her people, promising
prettily to love her lover just so,
for all the days of their lives.

Like she imagined she knew who she'd be forever.

Just after the honeymoon, that woman's first love
died alone—and with him that hopeful bride.
His sober toast at the wedding had ended with,
"Mom, seeing you together makes me believe."

She altered in an instant: face crazed
with new lines, grey hairs sprouting.

Her ringer stepped in to identify the body.
She rained kisses on the icy softness
of her prince's not-quite-sleeping face
as she'd done when he was three
and life was one game after another.

Back when she thought she'd die without more romance.

After kissing death, whose lips
did she bring home? I feel sorry now
for that sweet fool who believed
that at 50 she could dress like a princess
and step into a fairy tale forever.

As if happily ever after was ever the real end of any true story.

I DON'T KNOW HOW YOU DO IT

"Brave" is a brand
we sear onto those
with no choice
but to carry
the biggest burdens:
bulls in the ring with
knives in their backs,
Black women on the bus,
losers of limbs, survivors
of beatings and betrayals,
beasts forced to bear up
with a load we don't want
to imagine having to carry.

My son's death
didn't make me
brave; it broke me.
Those who praise
my strength seem
to be slyly critiquing
my grief performance.
Sentences starting,
"I could never…"
trip off a tinnitus
of siren sounds.

Sometimes I wish
I could wear a mark
to show the extent
of the damage, scars
to prove how twisted
and charred standing
in the fire left me,
but then strangers would
exclaim at how brave
I was to bear the branding,
tell me they could never
be doing as well as I am.

LIQUOR BOTTLE MIGHT AS WELL BE A PISTOL

by Kyle Fisher-Hertz, age 25

Liquor bottle might as well be a pistol;
I take shots like a cop with his clip full.
Fuck popping a pill—I need a fistful,
cuz the beast in my belly never gets full.

I try to stand my ground but I get pulled
like a midget with a leashed-up pit bull.
Cuz my addiction grips and then it yanks my chain.
Makes my thoughts so naughty I should spank my brain

Coming up with grand plans so damn insane
I'll break my arm like a retard, then go to the ER,
and tell the nurse "10" when I rank the pain.
Cuz I'll do anything it takes just to get my fix.
But when I start to sober up. I regret the shit.
Gotta figure out a plan to forget the shit.

So while I think, I pour a drink, just to wet my lips.
Next thing I know, I'm shooting dope, and I'm stressed as shit
cuz I'm digging in a vein I can't get to hit;
I'm fucked—and not just the tip,
fucked like an old lady with a busted hip.
I'm alone and I've fallen and I can't get up,
laid out on the couch feeling jammed as fuck,
exhausted by the thought of just standing up—

let alone trying to hustle up my next score.
Getting high's the only thing I get dressed for
or take breaths for.
I just press forward
with the piece of life
I traded all the rest for.

UNSOLICITED ADVICE

The day before my son died,
I tried to write a poem, which began:

Advice I Want to Give Today:
Get up early.
Go to the doctor
even if you don't have an appointment;
stay there until they help you.

I looked at those words,
realized they were a plea,
not a poem,
and gave up,
and practiced not giving advice
when no one was asking for it,
practiced sending silently
a message of faith,
practiced showing
I believed my son
knew how to take care of himself,
and thus didn't need my advice.

Or at least that was the message
my silence was supposed to send.

And right up until the call
telling me my son was dead,
I felt pretty proud of myself
for having managed for once
to keep my mouth shut
and my advice to myself.

EVERYTHING HAPPENS

Though not for any real reason.
People love to believe in destiny—
in fate giving their lives meaning—
even if their fate causes agony.

But what if everything happens
at random, no reason whatsoever.
Tragedies shake us, slap and
break us, leaving us crushed forever

with no explanation.
No one tells us the divine plan.
We weather amputations,
give up our games of kick the can

without ever knowing why.
No one stanches our inner bleeding.
We learn to parrot the great lie:
We're fine! In fact, we're succeeding.

People see what they want to see;
they see we're fine because they need
us to be. They swear prayer is the key.
God plans, we're in His hands. Why plead

for mercy? None will come. Perhaps
we like imagining God wanted all along
whatever befell us; in pain, gone numb,
if it's God's will, how can it be wrong?

BLACK AND WHITE

*"The way I look at addiction now is completely different. I can't tell you
what changed inside of me, but these are people... they need help."*
—Eric Adams,ex-narcotics cop turned treatment coordinator
"In Heroin Crisis, White Families Seek Gentler War on Drugs"
The New York Times, Oct. 30, 2015.

When your kids were addicts, we called them animals, junkies,
crack whores, superpredators, garbage.

When our kids were addicts, *The New York Times* labeled them
substance-use disordered, heralded their humanity.

When your kids were in pain, doctors didn't believe them,
so prescribed fewer narcotics.

When our kids were in pain, doctors didn't want them to suffer,
so doled out pills with largesse,

When your kids sold weed, their pled-down punishment included
permanent ineligibility from student loans.

When our kids sold rainbow bags of pills put out at parties, police
urged us to put them in treatment.

When your kids went to court, we buried them without a backward
glance, made up long minimums, three strikes.

When our kids went to court, judges bent over backward to get them
rehab, stayed sentences, clean records.

When your kids got caught with cocaine, entrepreneurially turned
into crack, we built more and bigger prisons.

When our kids got caught with cocaine—well, never mind, our kids
had no cops busting down their dorm doors.

No one threw our kids to the ground, kicked their legs apart, knelt on their necks when they protested.

Instead we wondered why our kids were throwing their good lives on the same trash heap as your kids.

We barely noticed how your kids' lives had been made dispensable, their futures trashed, until our kids started dying.

BARGAINING

AMERICAN THANKSGIVING, 2018

Everyone at our table,
except the 4-year-old,
is in some way drugged,
so probably for her,
it's merely a matter of time.

My mother is the only
obvious one, eyes pulled
three-quarters closed
by painkiller weights.

The rest of us float
on our normal mix
of antidepressants,
alcohol, marijuana,
anti-psychotics,
and tranquilizers.

The guest on anti-psychotics
needs his medley of meds
to still the voices in his head;
the one on tranquilizers
recently quit drinking,
so wants help to face the crowd
of avid onlookers she imagines.

That just leaves us pot smokers
who gather giggling over
a bowl in my basement before
tucking in to the tryptophan-
heavy meal. Nothing to see here.

Over dinner, giving thanks
for our abundance and each
other, we mourn my son,
who overdosed two years ago,
leaving us all mystified

as to why he couldn't
just learn to take his drugs
and keep suffering
like the rest of us.

REVERSING TIME

"The wheel begins its *if only* turning."
—Mary Jo Bang, *Elegy*

If I had one chance
to run your life in reverse;
how far back would I need to go
to change the ending?

I'd have to start the night you died:

You pull that last needle from your arm,
untie that last tourniquet,
stand up from the bathroom floor,
stuff the works back into your pocket,
walk backward out of that Best Western,
put your helmet back on, begin your bike ride
backward to the home you'd made at Grandma's,
stopping to return the heroin and meth to your dealer,
who gives back your money, then continuing
to where your daughter Maggie waits,
crying until you take her into your arms.

That wouldn't be far enough to save you, though
I'd need to keep rewinding three more years
to the night you tried crack, first drug
to fishhook you and yank down hard:

You put the loaded pipe and lighter down,
the nervous smile dies on your face
as you walk purposefully, backward, out
of that smoky room, leaving behind that man
holding out that pipe you'll never hit.
You make it backwards home, strip,
slide back into your lonely bed at midnight,
roll over and let yourself fall back asleep.

But to make your mind change that night,

I'd have to go back farther, early enough
to undo whatever made you think
you were smart enough to outsmart addiction,
yet not worthy of a good life, filled with love.

Where would I begin?

THINGS I DID THAT I IMAGINE KILLED MY SON

Had an abortion when I was 19.
Had an affair while married to his father.
Had enough of his need for rescue.

Left my marriage.
Left my son in public school.
Left him with his dad when he was 17.

Held on too tight.
Held him to impossible standards.
Held back my judgment.

Made partying look like fun.
Made light of his fears.
Made sure he felt my disappointment.

Told him the truth too often.
Told him lies all his life.
Told both of us everything would be OK.

Believed his lies.
Believed he could get better on his own.
Believed my love could save him.

MY LIFE IS A BORING TRAGEDY

by Kyle Fisher-Hertz, age 25

My life is a boring tragedy,
a tired parody of itself
collapsing dispassionately.

A current of hope rises
and falls like a sine wave,
but predictability strips the function

of any excitement or meaning—
even on the upswing—

and soon the rising
and falling hope is nothing more
than the breathing chest
of an old napping universe.

DUST

Since my son's cremation,
I sift through the ashes,
looking for what I missed.

There's the moment six years ago
he first told me he was on crack,
imagining a cure existed.

The moment before he'd announced
he was gay, maybe, tried blaming
shame for his need to self-destruct.

I tried to focus as his confessions
kept coming: that check-writing problem
had been a scam he'd tried to run.

That teaching job he'd loved found him
snorting coke in the boys' room,
all his money problems drugs.

In high school years, he reveals,
he met men in parks while pining for
a girlfriend, learning to hate himself.

Two years now he's dead,
and his ashes are spread
on mountains, buried in my yard,

funneled into a necklace
his girlfriend hung in her car,
the remainder saved

in case his daughter wants some.
All that's left of him's spread thin
as he was in life, believing

he couldn't ever be whole and happy.
I still don't know why he couldn't survive
once I was done keeping him alive.

COULD I HAVE KEPT YOU HERE?
An Italian Sonnet

What if you'd lived to be an old addict?
Stretched wide, hooded eyes giving you away
while the you I loved vanished day by day?
Clean sometimes 'til I'd think you had it licked...
How long, how much a hopeless derelict
would you have been before I couldn't say
I believed in you? How long 'til I'd pray
for you to go by any means you picked?

I'll never know, since you took my belief
you could think yourself well, use willpower
to build a life—proved you had a real disease
that needed meds to treat it, not just grief.
I wish I had been there in your last hour,
to say, "Wait, take the Suboxone now, please."

THE ONLY HIGH

For Steph by Kyle Fisher-Hertz, age 25

Long before I ever bought a legal drink,
I was punch-drunk off your laughter.

Girl, you've gotta be the only high I ever chased
that didn't lead me to disaster.

I kept chasing like a dog in a park full of squirrels
while you tried to hold my leash

'Til I wore you down and you let go
to let me be a beast released.

By the time I turned around you were already gone,
but you left a note with your number,

Sayin', "Call me; I'd still like to hear your voice,
but I can't watch you go under."

SLIDING DOORS

Gliding through the sliding doors
into the life I might have known:
You're still alive. You're 25.
I gave up love so you'd stay grown.

You live with me. You sleep 'til noon.
You break my heart (or so I think,
not knowing there what broken is).
You laugh, you breathe, you eat, you drink.

You Scrabble me. You lose your phone.
"You drive me crazy!" A foolish lie.
The life you're living seems the worst
because I haven't seen you die.

On this door's side, I'm no one's wife.
You're not misled about my heart,
don't dream I'd be OK without you,
think I'll die if you depart.

So you don't. You stay. You suffer through,
my martyrdom around your neck.
You hurt yourself and everyone else.
You leave a wake; your life's a wreck.

Would part of me if she could see
your hopeless march toward dissolution
choose this life I built without you?
Let you take my absolution?

What kind of mother would I be
keeping you here in misery?

The 1998 movie *Sliding Doors* depicts a woman having two different lives depending
on whether she makes it through a train's sliding doors on time.

MANY MOTHERS MAKE WORSE MISTAKES:

Pass down diseases,
mix up medications,
fail to forgive,
never learn how to love,
shoot up, shut down, crash cars,
call their children their cross to bear,
leave them alone, leave them behind,
demand devotion to a punishing God,
make them kneel on rice,
beat them 'til they black out.

I once ran a child-abuse prevention center,
halls echoing with the screams
of all the abuse we failed to prevent;
I saw firsthand the failures
and sicknesses visited upon the innocents.

Those broken children, the raped and scarred,
the crushed and made mad, continued to live.

So karma can't have killed my son.
The worst maternal errors
among the thousands I made
cannot warrant this permanent
parting, this destruction of hope
or any ability to make amends.

Yet still I am sorry, desperately
sorry, for each and every one.

PRESSURE RESISTANT

I tried to force my son to be a father,
but he resisted, insisted he could
Just Say No, he didn't want a baby
yet, wouldn't choose that woman
he'd made pregnant even if he did.

Everything else my son had done,
the student loans he spent on crack,
stealing from tills, taking our pills,
thieving bills from his sister's
treasure box—all could be forgiven.

But his failure to father
was a boulder
he couldn't sail around.

How had I raised
a deadbeat dad?
Month after month,
with photos, videos,
stories from my visits,
I browbeat that boy
into being there. Took
two years for him to
step up, but his daughter
took at once to reaching
for him, calling him
Dada, lighting up
at the sight of him.

And then, within
months, he was dead,
an overdose labeled
accidental.

Turns out
I couldn't force him
to be a father after all.

WITHOUT YOU

by Kyle Fisher-Hertz, age 24

Without you I'm so lonely
but when I'm with you I'm alone.
I lock my bedroom door,
open up my dresser drawer,
and start to swoon, smitten
seeing you in front of me.

Warm tingles spread out from my core.
God Damn! I couldn't want you more.
Who wouldn't want to be alone
with you for company?
You just please me, I just let you.
Selfishness does not upset you.
If you could talk to me you'd whisper,
"Please, abuse me."
Everyone tells me to forget you.
And some days my mind is set to,
but your voice echoes through my head,
"Come back and use me."

Will you destroy me? Maybe.
But you're not the problem, baby.
The issue's something else
I've tried to cover.
It's not you, it's me.
I'm sure a whore like you can see
My problem is I'm such a selfish lover.

ANOTHER MORNING BREAKS

Another morning breaks
my heart beating me back
from the wild hope

I thought you couldn't take,
back when my life was intact,
though I thought it broken.

Who knew I'd miss lying awake,
my mind careening over tracks
of fraying rope.

Who knew a fear I couldn't shake
would be a thing I'd want back?
Instead I have to cope

with knowing this call's not fake;
you did it: your last shot of smack
shot dead my last hope.

How can that have been the final take?
Rewind! Please. Don't fade to black
and leave my scope

magnifying each mistake
I made. No light can escape that crack.
You've sentenced me to grope

blindly, forever—with thirst I can't slake,
each new day adding weight to the pack
I must bear alone up this oily slope.

WHAT I SHOULD HAVE SAID

After my wedding, you relapsed,
came home from detox shaky,
called to seek my advice.

Wary of enabling you,
or enraging my weary wife,
I focused on logistics,
not your life, said your girlfriend
and daughter could stay with me,
said it seemed unfair for them
to be made homeless
by your failure to stay clean.

Ever reasonable, you agreed
this made sense, heard this
as a pass, knew they'd be safe,
so left them—and this life—behind.

I could hardly look at your girlfriend
in the weeks after, wanted nothing
to do with your desolate daughter,
covered the mirrors at home because
I could even less bear to look at myself.

How often and crazily now
I circle back to beg and bargain
for one more chance
to field that phone call—
one more chance to sacrifice
everyone else to save you.

So easy to see, once your disease
turned out to be terminal,
what I should have said:
        "Whatever you need to do
        to keep yourself alive."

COLD COMFORT

A friend who helped arrange my son's funeral
calls to ask if I'll speak to another mother
who lost her son to drugs—her fourth friend in
two years, she says, to lose a son to overdose.

My son is dead 29 months; I want to be helpful.
But nothing I say can ease this woman's pain.
Instead, I am the one who ends up weeping
as the woman recounts how, when her hand
and forearm were torn off by a washing machine
before pesky safety standards were imposed,
it took her three years to absorb the loss.

"But maybe the comparison doesn't hold up," she says,
"Losing a hand was so much easier than losing a child."

She tells me her son was home for a visit;
she had a bad feeling, wished she could stay home.
But he was 35, an addict more than half his life,
and her students, juvenile inmates, needed her
—so she went in. "And I know he'd be alive if
I'd taken the day off. I have to live with that."

I tell her my Number One piece of advice, one grieving mother to
another: Stop looking for what you could have done differently.

"No!" She pushes back. "I want to look at everything
I did so I can make different choices in the future."
Even though that was her only child. Even though
no other death will ever leave her searching
everywhere for just one more chance to get it right.

ECHO

Your ghost has come to live with us;
she's 3 and claims she remembers you.
She likes to tell people her daddy died,
because then they look at her with pity,
which she's learned to crave like candy.

Your ghost eats only sugar, chews
through her tooth decay, races, panting,
in figure-eights that floor us, demanding
unwavering attention, screaming, "Look
at me!" if we dare avert our gaze.

People think I must treasure her, must
be thrilled she's in our house, a do-over,
another chance—as if I'd ever want to
pour the love you left into a breakable
vessel already showing deep cracks.

Sometimes I speak of you: "Your daddy
liked chocolate, was afraid of horses,
loved spinning until he fell down," but
she has no interest yet in who you were,
only cares your death makes her special.

Your ghost sleeps in the room I wouldn't
let you live in, back when I foolishly feared
enabling you more than your death. She sleeps
face up, like you in your cheery childhood.
What good was the labor of those years—

and why would I want to repeat them?
I want back the blood that ran red in you,
not its halved replica running rampant here.
I want you back on the pedestal we built
before your failures felled you. I'd trade

all these days of play for one more day
with you. But I don't get to choose. Your ghost
has erased and replaced you, scratches at my door
each day at dawn, demands I be appeased
by learning to love what's left of you.

THAT MOMENT

by Kyle Fisher-Hertz, age 22

The first droplet of consciousness splashes the surface of a sublime dream, and awareness spreads through me like black ink in the pristine water of my mind. I pretend not to know that I am curled and alone beneath my blanket—desperately hurling anchors into the nebulous dream-world that is rapidly fading into obscurity. I squeeze my eyes shut, as if I could plug the drain and contain the fantasy leaking out of me, but all that is left is an out-of-focus film reel projecting a hazy memory onto the insides of my eyelids. I sigh, missing something I can't recall, fully aware that I now must face a reality that is not my own creation.

BEAUTIFUL BOY

As my son was descending toward the void,
I read David Sheff's book about his son,
named for the John Lennon song that later played
with the photo montage my friend created
for my son's funeral. Today my daughter and I
will see a movie by the same name as we try
to understand why some addicts live and some die.

If I'd had advice from Sheff himself
on what he's learned saves lives:
     "programs that don't require 12-step groups… that offer evidence-based care,
     psychological testing, treatment for co-occurring disorders, cognitive behavioral
     therapy, motivational interviewing, and addiction medication,"
I would not have been able to follow it.

Even the Make-A-Wish rehab we scored,
with its equine therapy, gym memberships,
beach volleyball, and ocean-view rooms,
still made everyone pray, go to meetings,
rewrite their steps, make repeated lists
of fears and resentments, tread endlessly
over the same lost ground. My son was too clever
to get a dual diagnosis, too smart for his own good.

The medication that kept him well for months
wasn't covered by Medicaid in most states.
Being cut off from my insurance when he turned 26
started his countdown clock: he was dead within three months.

Beautiful, beautiful, beautiful boy.
How hard it is to learn
we knew nothing
about what could save you
until you were already gone.

For Sheff's advice, see: https://drugfree.org/parent-blog/when-my-son-became-addicted-i-thought-it-was-his-problem-but-addiction-is-a-family-disease/

FOR AMBER

by Kyle Fisher-Hertz, age 26

If you're convinced that the words I whisper into your ear
are a calculated product of the game I spit,
then don't waste your time watching them spill onto this page.
Then every "I love you" that has ever come stamped
out of my core to you ought to be penned up
and viewed warily as a herd of Trojan horses
in which I encapsulate my manipulation.
Then you should purge every piece of myself
I've ever shared with you,
because they're all poisoned with a hidden agenda.

And yet.

You take my shared pieces inside you.
You bask in the "I love yous."
You do watch my words.
You hold them up to a light like a diamond or a 100 euro note.
You realize you'd never know the difference between genuine
and counterfeit, and you sigh and toss them into a box
that is either filling with treasure or trash.

The day you drag that box to the curb
and send it off to be buried in a landfill of cynicism,
it's trash, no matter what's inside it.

But as long as you cherish it,
and keep it somewhere safe and special,
then you live your life with a hidden treasure.

That is all I can offer you. A treasure chest you have to believe in.
I read the worry in your eyes. The fears that you are guarding a fool's gold.
Well, what is a lover if not a fool?
It is insane to love completely. Delusional.
But it is a delusion we get to create together.

My treasure box full of your love
is worth more than anything
I could ever hold in my hand.
You have one, too.
We are rich within our lovers' kingdom.
Stay with me, and we'll never want for anything.

DON'T GO

Too late to tell my son, already gone,
but still time to say to you, mother
of my son's child: Please don't go.

I know they're loud, the voices
that make you believe nobody
loves you nor ever will, but look:

I have been with you since before
the baby came, irritating you, like
a pearl, with my terrible judging,

And still you can't get rid of me,
no matter how you bare your teeth
at me, snarling from against the wall.

I have come on my knees, palms up,
to lure you out from beneath the house,
to say I see you burying your longing,

I need your forgiveness for every
judgment of myself I project
onto you; I pray to hear your breath

slow to normal. Please, stay, peel away
the piles you hide behind, rest in my arms,
take for yourself the love my son left.

VEGAS

by Kyle Fisher-Hertz, age 24

In desert heat,
devil's deceit
creates a dark oasis.

No rules decreed
and fools are freed
to try on different faces.

Barroom fights
and naked nights
where only masks are worn.

Girls and guys
live in disguise,
identities adorned.

Passing through
a time or two,
you might come out the same.

But if you stay
you'll find a way
to lose the you who came.

FORENSIC EXAMINATION

I lay out the photos chronologically,
birth to death, looking for the one
that will leap up shouting, "Here! This
is the day you might have saved him!"

Instead they just tell their happy story:
loved baby, loved boy, ever joyful.
When his face shut down at 12, only
hindsight lets me see my disruptive
need to leave his father shatter him,
corrupting his fierce faith in love.
In uprooting him, I showed him
he could be switched with a flip
from popular golden child
to nervous nerd who couldn't
tell a joke nor make a single friend.

I rushed him back, replanted him
in familiar soil where he seemed
to thrive again, but by then he had seen
how powerless he was, knew his good life
could collapse anytime. The worm biding its time
squirmed out of its hole as my son learned
his good life was towers waiting to fall.

Pictures after adolescence barely
show a glitch; he still hams it up, skates
past his drug arrests. He rock climbs,
goes to college, falls in love, teaches, hikes.

He leaves no photos of himself on crack,
nothing in his journals about the men he met
through Grindr, no evidence of how he gradually
ground himself down every time he felt good.
In his last pictures, he holds his daughter,
wraps his arms around me, dances with his sister,
gazes into his girlfriend's eyes, pushes his grandmother's
wheelchair, worm rolling under his tongue.

My compulsive need to find an explanation
keeps me poring over pictures, videos, poems
for years. Now I've excavated all my mistakes—
and found only this: nothing brings him back.

ACCEPTANCE
& FINDING
MEANING

THANKSGIVING, 2002

By Kyle Fisher-Hertz, age 11

Thanks for my sister, my mom, and my dad
Thanks for all the fun times I've had
Thanks for all the relatives from Vegas to Denmark
Thanks for the warmth of the light and the beauty of the dark
Thanks for all the food I have and the clothes I can afford
Thanks for all the toys I have so I'm hardly ever bored.
Thanks for all the open arms that love me every day.
Thanks for my acceptance of all whether straight or gay.
Thanks for all the people from Afghanistan to Iraq
Thanks for letting us be thankful
                    and have others be thankful back.

RELIQUARY

My life serves as a reliquary
for my son's.

Since he died, I hold each
precious relic reverently

uplifted so his bones shine
just right under the lights.

I rub to glowing the treasures
made or made up,

the memories misrembered
or recalled sharply as stars.

My home serves as a feretory
for my son.

Since he died, I've fossilized
his papers, ordered them

in ways they'd never been.
I wrote a book of him.

His poems have place of honor
on these pages, this tome

a shrine for my son where I would sit
you to rewatch with me

his every radiant moment, moment
by moment, our hearts

hammering with wonder and dread
for knowing the end in advance.

I can't ask that of you, so my life must do
as a reliquary for his.

What more can I do to lift him
from his early grave?

I NEVER WANTED MY FORTUNE TOLD

You are 17, home
with me and your sister
for a Mother's Day buffet
at the Hotel Northampton.
After the sumptuous meal,
we people-watch, play
Scrabble, squabble, giggle.
You beat me, as usual.

Such a lovely day,
I announce we'll
make it a tradition,
eat here every year
for Mother's Day!

You are never home
again for that holiday,
never go to that buffet
with me again. I try
going without you
but by then can't
keep anything down.

The card you gave me
has a recording, you
and your sister sing-songing:
"Happy Mother's Day, Ma;
we love you!" before the song
"You're Unbelievable" bursts out.

What might I have done differently
had I known that would be the last
card not filled with your apologies?

Not a thing. It's a sweet memory,
made sweeter because I had no idea
of all the troubles that lay ahead.

CROCODILE

By Kyle Fisher-Hertz, age 24

[According to Hindu belief,]
"The alchemy of energy teaches that death will always yield new life."

So why when the crocodile snaps its jaws
closed on the unsuspecting fawn bent down for a drink
do we only recoil and pity the young deer's untimely death,
never celebrating the life being digested within the croc's belly?

The laws of physics teach that energy can be neither destroyed nor created,
and yet as the dying soldier breathes his last breath,
the medic looking into his eyes would swear to the physicist
that he has seen the destruction of energy.

Perhaps the answer lies in the laws of entropy teaching us the lesson
we all already know, that as surely as time moves forward,
the universe becomes ever more chaotic.

That the deer becomes the crocodile and never the other way around.

THE BODY'S EXPRESSION

Our bodies manifest the pain
our words cannot contain.

I.
When my son was an infant
I couldn't express my milk
and grew engorged;
my soft flesh turned stony,
any touch excruciating,
no cure but ice.
I wept with longing
to be home nursing,
bathroom pumping
a one-day outlet
that made me miss more
the antidote I craved,
which was not expression
by pump, but my baby back
in my arms, on my breast
longer than six weeks.

My latest maternal pain
also turns me to stone;
still not expression I want,
just my baby back. Instead,
my body finds new outlets.

Motion keeps the pain
at bay: the herniated disc,
the blade-divided heart,
both muted by distraction.
Only when I stand still
do grief's pincers seize
my lower back, clamp
the spot where my neck
meets my shoulder,
rip my meal back out

through my gasping mouth.

The miracle is: I will be able
to absorb my son's death,
just not all at once. My breasts
had one day to dry up, don armor,
get back to a job they didn't want.
What lies beneath them, my enlarged
heart, is a damaged muscle; she won't
work well against her will; even
pumping double-time she can't fill,
then empty in so great a hurry.

The needle is in, but speeding
the plunger would kill me. Sometimes
I still need the walls to hold me up.

I've been making my way, delicately,
one memory at a time, trying to digest
all the moments that brought us here,
chewing each misstep mindfully,
remembering to breathe between bites,
so the glass is smooth when it goes down,
so I can forgive each choice I made.

Sometimes I forget to pace myself,
and the whole truth rushes in at once,
every mistake I made playing at warp
speed on the zoetrope in my head
until my body rejects the rushing
influx forcefully enough to scare me.

My stiff neck asks how it can ever
turn easily to face this full-on.
I've been crawling out of my skin,
wishing to be out of this body
before the full brunt bears down.
No wonder I tear tiny wounds,
scratching at the backs of my hands.

However saddled, here I am;
the six weeks this body fed my son
are the only ones I will ever get;
the lifetime I have left in this body
is all the time I'll ever have
to love my son with every cell.
For that alone, I must continue.

II
To satisfy my worried wife,
to keep the will to live this life,
I smooth on creams, take
medicines, see doctors,
even though I know there is
nothing in me they can fix.

What can a stranger do to treat
the wind-rush of pain I breathe in
upon waking? When my heart presses
out until the membranes near rupture,
it's up to me to release air from the valve
by breathing in. Then out. All day.

I look at lists of fears
my son's sponsor
ordered him to write:
> "That God is a lie
> I tell myself,
> that I will die
> without doing anything
> I hoped to get done."

I resolve to write a list
of hopes instead,
just as soon as hope
comes back to me.

NATURAL WONDERS

I once took my kids
on a cross-country adventure,
by which I mean,
I loaded up our car, left their
father and my jobs, and ran up
years of credit-card debt.

That trip, those memories
of white-water rafting
the Rio Grande, of
seeing them see
the Grand Canyon
for the first time,
of the candle-lit
courtyard in Santa Fe
where we ate Mexican
then strolled to our hotel;
of Dollywood, the natural
bridge and all the other
wonders—for these I am glad
debt was recklessly encouraged
in the early aughts. I'd never
take on that burden now, having felt
its weight shut down
my choices for a decade.

Still, my memories have multiplied in value
now that I can never make new ones,
which makes me glad we had those weeks
with only the landscape and each other
on our way to my blowing up all our lives.

FOR THOSE WHO NEED SCIENCE BEFORE FAITH

1.   Field Study

I once had a childish theory all souls were connected
by invisible wires that could be stretched but never snapped.

The closer two people, the thicker the strand I suspected
ran between them—like phone cables able to grow and adapt.

When I grew up and had children, my theory was subjected
to field study as their braided cables twined and overlapped

with mine, then each other's. Their spirits arrived unaffected
by doubt; they gazed at me with unfounded trust, utterly rapt.

My theory now seemed fact. My exposed soul spilled unprotected
into theirs. Our shared joints soldered closed; our fused pipelines were mapped.

2.   Microchimerism

Turns out there are scientific names for my long-suspected
concepts: Microchimerism posits fetal cells are apt

to switch sides—so an embryo's unique cells are injected
into its mother, while hers spin the skin in which baby's wrapped.

Older siblings' cells linger in the mom, then are projected
into future children—which means my son's particles stay trapped

in me and his kid sister, even though he disconnected.
His DNA lives on in us, though his lifeline has been snapped.

Our swapped cells may explain why, when my children were dejected,
their pain overwhelmed me; my face caught fire if theirs was slapped.

3.   Quantum entanglement

In quantum physics, entanglement theory is accepted
proof that some bonds can never be severed. If a photon's zapped

in two, its split bits act as one no matter where detected
(though they hide this parlor trick if a photo lens is uncapped).

My son's first deity fell when I proved human; he'd expected
my perfection, found cracks in all my walls. Angry, he unwrapped

and trashed his greatest gifts: brilliance, faith, love, hope. Disaffected,
he died praying to believe. We fell down with him, thunder-clapped

by grief, our spirits pulsing toward his dead end, misdirected
into doubting we had souls—or else how could he have relapsed?

4.   Post-Traumatic Growth

Long before he learned quantum theories, my son respected
God; he believed without thinking. Cynicism handicapped

him, led his sister to mimic his scorn—'til unexpected
loss tore our shells clean off, left us shivering, terrified, sapped

enough for the hardest lesson: grief comes to reconnect us.
Each tragedy tears off a veil. Spiritually, we'd napped

through our lives, unhumbled. The skepticism we'd erected
was unwinding our frayed strands. Then Post-Traumatic Growth remapped

our wires, pushed us back toward Love. My son's cord is inflected,
not cut. I must trust our pipes still flow, our connection left intact.

UNPLUGGED

A Poem for his sister, Jamie, then 22, by Kyle Fisher-Hertz, age 24

Pipelines emanating from our respective centers
allow now to be entered collectively.
Seven billion perspectives become one
where the pipelines meet,
our thoughts circulating like blood
pumped by a universal heartbeat.

And in this web of pipes, infinitely tangled
you and I, of course, were angled
side-by-side, adjacently connected
so close that pieces of our souls
are shared through direct injection,
our pipes flowing and our love growing,
becoming ourselves together,

So when toxic tar like a starless night sky
began to clog my pipeline,
nothing had a shot of getting through
except for you.
The chatter of the universe was muted.
I was a numb appendage, cut-off circulation
at risk of amputation.

And so you pleaded through the pinhole
of connectedness that remained
for me to unplug the gunk, recirculate myself,
and love myself like you love me.

LEARNING TO LIVE TOGETHER

Grief settles in for another winter,
smug and comfy. He scatters photos.
replaces my reading, hogs the remote.
I can't make him leave because
he's holding my son hostage. Without
Grief, I'll never see my son again—

so I let him stay, but he invades
my space, makes faces at me,
shoves me out of bed at 4:45 a.m.—
the time my son died, he reminds me,
as if I need reminding. I can't stand
when he's mean like that, a bore, repeats

himself, rubs it in. He can be rough, too:
sucker-punching me with a sudden,
searing memory. No apologies ever,
even when he lies. Yet sometimes
when I'm lonely, I want to pull Grief
closer, rub on him, drown in his essence.

I know how cruel he can be, how empty
I feel when we spend time together.
Yet still I'm always thinking of him.
Sometimes he pretends to be kind,
lets me think I'll be joining the party,
then leans in to whisper slyly,

Look who's missing, just as everyone
else starts to sing. He makes sure
I never forget for a minute, jabbers on
even when I'm talking. I've accepted
he's here to stay, though I hope someday
he's going to take it a little easier on me.

THE SPEED OF LIFE

The whole thing went by
in the blink of an eye
yet crawled along
at a painstaking pace—
leaving me wowed then
weary as my son moved
from snuggly, stuffed-up boy,
eyes always following me,
to furious teen who did
chores so poorly, it was
easier never to ask his help.

Remembering I had a right
to a life of my own was
roughest in the early years,
which is how time both
crawled and raced by me,
one foot in my future, one
on the diaper pail.
Feminist pride pushed me
to pay some mind at times
to my own desires. Now
I can take all the time
in the world to regret this.

The years since my son's
death are piling on,
going fast and slow.
He is still, always,
26, but now his sister
is two years past that,
grown up overnight in
our four years of hard-fought,
minute-by-minute surviving.

We try to stay focused on today,
the only way to wind up
with a life that moves
at love's pace.

A LESSON FROM AMANDA PALMER'S PODCAST
A Petrarchan Sonnet

The darkness brings forth incredible fruit,
says the radio voice, speaking of seeds
planted in pain; growing tall over weeds,
bearing juicy crops for us to transmute.
Do we want this abundance? Well, that's moot;
hard growth is how grief expresses its needs.
Taking over brush or pen, it impedes
our left brains, pulls at truths we must uproot.

How lucky those artists dabbling in light,
their poems vague and pretty, their paintings bland.
They haven't yet been pummeled to their knees
so they don't know we have to dig all night
to reach whatever anguish brought to hand.
They still choose fruit by giving it a squeeze.

ACCEPTANCE

Spent so many days in desperation,
searching for a strategy, a savior,
the one thing I must have missed
to bring you back from the brink,

that when you died, I kept right on
searching, even amped up operations,
knowing there must be something I forgot,
some way to go back, rescue you before

you killed yourself. More than four years
of daily yoga later, I just let out the breath
I've been holding. Oh. I see. It's over;
there's nothing left for me to do

except keep right on loving you.

THE BURN MOSAIC

In Yellowstone
the dead stand among the living,
towering aisles of eyeless sentinels
gazing over God's toppled pick-up sticks,
ashen, leafless, lifeless stands,
empty arms reaching skyward
amid forestfuls of bright, green upstarts.

It can take 100 years for a burned-out tree
to disintegrate. Meanwhile, life
does not stop for fire; all the unscorched
seeds still struggle toward the sun.

In Yellowstone,
no woods are free of fallen trunks
nor new-growth pole pines.
Dead silver stands make a feeding ground
for bugs, a den for snakes,
a hiding place for breathless prey.

Park signs tell of The Burn Mosaic:
fires rip open empty space
for sunlight to bathe the ground;
ash nourishes the earth, meadows
are born, saplings thrive, flowers find air,
pine cones burst to spill new life.

In Yellowstone, signs fail to mention
the charred bodies of woodland creatures
left littering the landscape, the millions
of dens and nests destroyed.

From a distance, fire weaves a tapestry.
Up close, a lone wolf whimpers, paws
the seared ground in search of her pups.

RIGHT HERE

by Kyle Fisher-Hertz, age 26

I hear the echo of a giggle
when I pray, "God, show yourself to me."
I think I may just be hearing a
reverberating chuckle bouncing off my skull
emanating from my cynical cerebral
cortex, uppity neurons sneering at my
search for something holy.

But then again
maybe it is You laughing at me.
Not the condescending laugh of a
physicist whom I ask to give me a
deep tissue massage with neutrinos,
but the gentle laugh of a mother laying
eyes on the wide panicked eyes of the
baby boy in her arms searching for his
mother's gaze.

"Shh, shh, shh," as you rock me.
"I'm right here. I've always been right here."

MY MOTHER KNOWS DEATH AND ITS LESSONS

"Life is pain and the enjoyment of love is an anesthetic."
—Cesare Pavese

My mother and Death are on a first-name basis.
She was still in grade school when her father
fell to lung disease, still a teen when her first
husband killed himself, still in her 20s when
her second daughter died of pneumonia, just
into her 30s when her ex-roommate was slain
in a murder-suicide, and just out of her 30s
when her brother wheezed his last breath.
Her mother died when she was in her 40s;
her last husband's congested heart failed her
when she was in her 50s; and her best friend
was killed by swift-moving cancer in their 60s,
six years before her only grandson overdosed
while living with her. Nearly every old love
she's found online turned up dead, too, along
with a beloved boss, decapitated at a stoplight.

If you were superstitious, you might call my mother
a jinx or death's harbinger. But she's a cheery woman
who collects Coca-Cola memorabilia and wears sequins
and light-up earrings. Her life's goal is to have more fun
and give every new baby a gift inscribed with its name.
She still spends her time dieting and critiquing
celebrity weight gains, tempted by QVC pitches,
insisting she doesn't give the big question of life
after death a thought, wants only a whiter smile and
towels to match the Betty-Boop theme in her bathroom.

I see now her focus on the frivolous conceals more
brilliance than it first reveals. If life is pain, and death
keeps gutting you, what else to do but look for laughs
and a chance to deliver delight with personalized gifts?
What more magic could she have wrung from within
the shadows death kept casting across the decades?
I bow now to the mirages she made glimmer in the dark.

I FEAR THAT MY PRAYERS

by Kyle Fisher-Hertz, age 26, one month before he died

I fear that my prayers are just waves sent out into the vast abyss,
rippling through space that might as well be emptiness...

Fear is the absence of faith,
and I am a scared little boy.
I fear the darkness,
yet I refuse to open my eyes to the light
convinced that my eyelids are all that is real.

As I stumble around stubbing my toes and bumping my head
with my eyes squeezed shut,
you tell me to open my eyes, for God's sake.
Don't I know how much easier it is to navigate life in the light?

CONTRIBUTING

At 26, I begged my 45-year old
husband please let me stay home
with our babies a year or two.
He insisted we couldn't afford it.

Ten years later, I stopped asking
permission, quit my job, took loans,
went back to school, left him there,
complaining of unequal contributions.

I worked 15 more years before my
firstborn died, after which my wish
was granted. My wife saw my need,
got a raise, refinanced, drew up a budget.

I miss giving extravagant gifts, traveling,
donating, but nothing worth working for.
My daughter, before becoming anti-capitalist,
resented my being home, asked don't I miss

making a contribution? My secret is:
I no longer wake each day wishing I hadn't.
I write, read, make love, cook, play;
I contribute by being glad to be alive.

BREAKING DOWN AT CAPE NEDDICK

Pebble Cove is a stretch of striped stones—
what our beaches looked like eons ago
before the endlessly patient waves stroked
the rocks into soft, fine-grained submission.

Each stripe in each rock is made of the matter
that makes us, matted down to a thin strip of
circling color wrapped around a cold egg shape.
Each a reminder of our place in the eternal

turning in the eras before commerce, before
gathering, before fish, in the cold infinity in which
there was rock and this water pulled up by the tireless
moon, then cast out, a glittery net floating down.

The tide like a deep breath draws in slowly, sifts
through its jewels, slides over whales and coral
and seaweeds all waving, waving as the net drags by,
settles to the bottom, pauses, turns, pulls back.

My chest opens wide to hold the salt air.
The steadfast waves rise up and slam down
against the immutable rocks, foaming
with frustration at all they haven't been able to break.

LIST OF HOPES

I didn't believe
after my son died
that I could ever hope
for anything again.

Yet I now have more hope
than when I was consumed
by terror over what new way
he'd find to hurt himself.

I hope my granddaughter
is allowed back
into our loving embrace
before she's grown.

I hope the children created
by my son's sperm donations
(four who know me so far!)
carry forward the best of him.

I hope my daughter
continues to inspire children
and activists and us,
her wildly proud parents.

I hope my wife and I celebrate
many joyous anniversaries
despite the shadow of sorrow
my son's death cast over us.

I hope this book
finds its way
into your hopeless hands
just when you need it most.

Afterword

I believe poetry can save lives, but as you can see, it couldn't save my son's. He was a brilliant, popular, well-loved boy who wrote slam poetry, jokes and songs with me and his little sister in our family poetry circles. He was also an accomplished young man, performing comedy in clubs across the country and on television in adolescence and teaching fourth graders math through the City Year program in his early 20s. He climbed Mt. Ranier, was a devoted son, grandson and brother, and was beloved by many as a kind, funny, attentive friend. He wrote love sonnets and prided himself on being a sensitive, romantic boyfriend.

Then, suddenly, he wasn't any of those things most of the time; being an addict became his life's full-time preoccupation. The endless circle he ran—relapsing, getting clean, relapsing—consumed the last three years of his life. He died at age 26 of an overdose of heroin and meth and left behind a two-and-a-half-year-old daughter he'd only known for six months.

The poems in this collection were written from the depths of my grief as I sought and failed to save my son, as I searched for a way to go on—and then as I fought and (so far) failed to be allowed to see my son's daughter Maggie, whose mother stopped letting any of Kyle's family members see or speak to his daughter in 2019. Knowing that Kyle was one of hundreds of thousands of Americans to die of an overdose in the mid-2010s, and that many grandchildren are cruelly cut off from loving grandparents after a parent dies, has not made my losses any easier, but publicly sharing my grief has. I am grateful for the support I received during the slow recovery these poems recount.

I feel fortunate my son left behind poems I've been able to include here, and I hope that reading our poetry offers some comfort to any of you struggling as we did and still do:

> • You are not alone if an out-of-order death has left you questioning everything you thought you knew.
> • You are not alone if you've loved someone extraordinary and watched drugs turn them into a stranger.
> • You are not alone if drugs have swallowed whole the person you were and still hope to be; please know there is hope in medication-assisted treatment, something we wish we'd understood in time.

- You are not alone if you are a loving grandparent no longer allowed to see your grandchildren; I'm sorry for all of us who have been cut off without reason.
- You are not alone if grief has ravaged you and left you for dead.
- You are not alone if you've eventually lifted your head and looked around to find the world is still beautiful.

By practicing self-care every day like it's your most important job, you can learn to carry grief on your hip, an extra weight that will always pull you slightly off balance. Even with this weight, post-traumatic growth can help you fight your way back to a new wholeness so that your limp will be barely detectable.

Thank you for reading these words and remembering Kyle and his daughter Maggie with me.

Acknowledgments

I am grateful for the prior publication of the following poems:

"All Our Hope Got Us Here"	*Tigershark Online Magazine, Issue 25*
"American Thanksgiving, 2018"	*Center for New Americans Anthology 2018*
"Another Morning Breaks"	*Silkworm 2019: Survival*
"Before We Were Afraid Our Son Would Rob Us"	*Blue Collar Review, Fall 2018*
"The Body's Expression"	*Please See Me—Spring Issue (07)*
"Breaking Down at Cape Neddick"	*Gyroscope Review, 2021 Spring, Sixth Anniversary Issue*
"For Those Who Need Science Before Faith"	*The Amethyst Review: New Writing Engaging with the Sacred, June 6, 2021*
"My Mother Knows Death"	*Silkworm 2020: Luck*
"Our First Date" by Kyle Fisher-Hertz	*Silkworm 2021: Rise*
"Reversing Time"	*Misfit Magazine, issue #32*
"Unplugged" by Kyle Fisher-Hertz	*The Amethyst Review, ibid*
"What I Should Have Said"	*Please See Me, ibid*
"Zombie"	*Silkworm 2021: Rise*

My heart is filled with gratitude for the wonderful, talented women and one great man who read through and offered enormously helpful constructive feedback on various iterations of this manuscript, including poet and author Dina Friedman, poet and teacher Janet Bowdan, and poet and translator

Michael Goldman. I am also thankful for the encouragement and excellent reviews the book received from poet, anthology editor, and children's book author Lesléa Newman, novelist Jacquelyn Mitchard, Board President of the Bereaved Parents of the USA Kathy Jenkins Corrigan, my dear friend Barbara Upton, my extraordinarily talented and enthusiastic daughter Jamie Fisher-Hertz, and my superlatively supportive wife Renee Sweeney. In addition, I am thankful for the ongoing encouragement I've received from my regular writing partners Elaine Thomas and Gina Rodriguez and from the many exquisite poets and writers with whom I have worked through Straw Dog Writers Guild, the Florence Poets Society, and the 30 Days of Poetry writers who write with me every November in support of the Center for New Americans. Finally, my deepest thanks to all those friends and family members who mourn and miss Kyle with me, especially Kyle's devoted father, Larry Hertz, and Kyle's grandmother, my mother, Gail Perry.

Lanette Sweeney's fiction, essays and poetry have appeared in *Rattle, Foliate Oak Review, Blue Collar Review, Please See Me,* several editions of the popular women's studies anthology *Women: Images and Reality,* and in many other publications. She taught writing and Women's Studies at SUNY New Paltz, where she earned her degrees, a BA in Women's Studies and an MA in English Literature in her 30s. Sweeney also worked as a college fund-raiser, non-profit executive, cocktail waitress, and real-estate agent. She is now a full-time writer thanks to her wife's support.